AF684805

The Myth of a Guilty Nation

The Myth of a Guilty Nation

BY

Albert Jay Nock
("historicus")

Ludwig von Mises Institute
AUBURN, ALABAMA

Originally published in 1922 by B. W. Huebsch, Inc.

Published in 2011 by the Ludwig von Mises Institute.

Published under the Creative Commons Attribution License 3.0.
http://creativecommons.org/licenses/by/3.0/

Ludwig von Mises Institute
518 West Magnolia Avenue
Auburn, Alabama 36832

Ph: (334) 844-2500
Fax: (334) 844-2583

mises.org

10 9 8 7 6 5 4 3 2 1

ISBN: 978-1-61016-238-8

Introduction

by Anders Mikkelsen

Albert Jay Nock wrote one of the first American books of WWI Revisionism—revising the received story of why WWI began. As a lover of history, what is particularly fascinating about his book *The Myth of a Guilty Nation* is not whether this is the best explanation for WWI. What is fascinating is the great contrast Nock makes between two wholly different views of the origin of the war. What "everyone knew" about the origins of The Great War at the time are quite different from what "everyone knows" now.

The common American notion was that Germany was responsible for the war. No less a personage than David Lloyd George declared "What are we fighting for? To defeat the most dangerous conspiracy ever plotted against the liberty of nations; carefully, skilfully, insidiously, clandestinely planned in every detail, with ruthless, cynical determination."

By reading the book we start to see just how differently people viewed the origin of the war at the time, especially in the U.S. Since WWI the revisionists won many of the battles, WWI is usually viewed today more as a tragedy, a pointless disaster, the effect of secret diplomacy, general militarism, etc. The reader today is therefore unaware of how many Americans understood the war as the sole outcome of a German conspiracy for plunder. While today we know Europe was an armed camp, the pro-allied propaganda claimed that Europe was unprepared for war. Nock makes the reader aware of the great extent to which the allied politicians continually lied to blame Germany and justify the war, or at least told stories with no regard for the truth. No wonder Hitler found British propaganda so inspiring. In fact the story at the time made it sound like Germany was trying to over-run Europe the way Hitler temporarily did a few decades later.

What Nock brings to the fore is the extent to which WWI may be viewed as the opposite of a conspiracy by Germany. If there was a conspiracy it would have been by the allied Entente powers. To a large degree it was blundered into by state officials, whose desire for peace was fatally undermined by their imperialist ambitions.

We should first note that he also touches on how many powerful parties simply wanted peace. However, small powerful parties in France,

Britain, and Russia all pushed for war and created secret treaties amongst each other. As Ralph Raico pointed out, English foreign policy was dominated by a small, secret clique no more answerable to Parliament and the people than a dictatorship like Nazi Germany. Those who knew of England's secret obligations lied to Parliament and denied their existence.

As Nock shows, English, French and Russian foreign policy was directed against Germany and Austria-Hungary, and military spending was quite large, and much greater than Germany and Austria-Hungary's. All three had powerful cliques who were aggressive towards the Central Powers. They were bound by secret treaties, though this alliance was not publicly acknowledged.

In Nock's book, this is roughly what happened to start WWI: Serbia and the Balkans had a foreign policy dominated by Russia. The assassins of Archduke Ferdinand were linked to the Russian pro-war clique. Russia had been "test" mobilizing since the spring of 1914, and its army alone was equal to Germany and Austria-Hungary combined. Russia had a secret treaty with France calling for France to support Russia if Russia mobilized and went to war. The UK had a secret treaty with France calling for it to support France during war, and to a much lesser but important degree, Russia. Bound by secret treaties all three powers found themselves thrust into war. Germany saw itself encircled by superior numbers. (Therefore it had to defeat France and Russia in decisive battles before it succumbed in a war of attrition. Similar to Israel's situation when faced with a land war against three neighbors.)

The assassination of the Archduke Ferdinand, conveniently for the Pro-War Entente cliques, set off the train of powder to the powder keg of a general European war of France, Russia and England against Germany and Austria-Hungary.

For sources Nock makes great use of Belgian diplomatic correspondence, which noted little evidence of German aggression. The Soviet Union also released many embarrassing secret documents from the Tsarist archives. Nock highly recommends English Liberals Francis Neilson's and E. D. Morel's works of WWI revisionism. (Neilson's *How Diplomats Make War* is hard to read, while Nock's is a breeze. Neilson focuses more on how English and other nations' diplomats created uncertainty.) It should be noted too that Nock shows evidence that Belgian neutrality was a fig leaf to justify unpopular UK involvement.

Having documentation of a push for war by cliques in Russia, France, and England, Nock shows how German war guilt is a myth and, if anything, pro-war cliques in Russia, France, and England were successful in conspiring for war.

What makes this book worth reading is not whether this is the best explanation for WWI. It is worth seeing how small groups of state officials engaged in secret actions that lead to a catastrophic war, and continually lied throughout the whole process to provide themselves ideological cover. What is fascinating is the great contrast Nock makes between two wholly different views of the origin of the war. While history and reality seem settled and known, people at different times have radically different understandings of the exact same events.

July 2011
New York City

Preface

THIS book is made up of a series of articles originally published in the *Freeman*. It was compiled to establish one point and only one, namely: that the German Government was not solely guilty of bringing on the war. I have not been at all concerned with measuring the German Government's share of guilt, with trying to show that it was either great or small, or that it was either less or more than that of any other Government or association of Governments. All this is beside the point. I do not by any means wish to escape the responsibility of saying that I think the German Government's share of guilt in the matter is extremely small; so small by comparison with that of the major Powers allied against Germany, as to be inconsiderable. That is my belief, demonstrable as I think by such evidence as has now become available to any candid person. But this has nothing whatever to do with the subject-matter of this volume. If the guilt of the German Government could be proved to be ten times greater than it was represented to be by the publicity-bureaux of the Allied Powers, the conclusion established in the following chapters would still remain. Guilty as the German Government may have been; multiply by ten any estimate that any person, interested or disinterested, informed or uninformed, may put upon its guilt; the fact remains that it was far, very far indeed, from being the only guilty party concerned.

If there were no practical end to be gained by establishing this conclusion, if one's purpose were only to give the German Government the dubious vindication of a *tu quoque*, the effort would be hardly worth making. But as I say at the outset, there is at stake an extremely important matter, one that will unfavourably affect the peace of the world for at least a generation—the treaty of Versailles. If the German Government may not be assumed to be solely responsible for the war, this treaty is indefensible; for it is constructed wholly upon that assumption. It becomes, not a treaty, but a verdict pronounced after the manner of Brennus, by a superior power which, without regard to justice, arrogates to itself the functions of prosecutor, jury and judge.

It is probably superfluous to point out that this treaty, conceived in the pure spirit of the victorious Apache, has, in practice, utterly broken down. It has not worked and it will not work, because it sets at defiance certain economic laws which are as inexorable as the law of gravitation. The incidence of these laws was well understood and clearly foretold, at the time of the peace-conference, by an informed minority in Europe, notably by Mr. Maynard Keynes in his volume entitled *The Economic Consequences of the Peace.* In this country also, a minority, sufficiently informed to know its right hand from its left in economic affairs, stood aghast in contemplation of the ruinous consequences which it perceived as inevitable under any serious attempt to put this vicious instrument into operation. But both here and in Europe, this minority was very small and uninfluential, and could accomplish nothing against the ignorant and unreasoning bad temper which the politicians kept aflame.

The treaty had therefore to go to the test of experiment; and of the results of this, one need surely say nothing, for they are obvious. The harder Germany tried to fulfill the conditions of the treaty, and the nearer she came to doing so, the worse things went in all the countries that were presumably to benefit by her sacrifice. The Central Empires are, as the informed minority in all countries has been from the beginning anxiously aware, the key-group in the whole of European industry and commerce. If they must work and trade under unfavourable conditions, they also thereby automatically impose correspondingly unfavourable conditions upon the whole of Europe; and, correspondingly unfavourable conditions are thereby in turn automatically set up wherever the trade of Europe reaches—for example, in the United States. There is now no possible doubt about this, for one has but to glance at the enormous dislocations of international commerce, and the universal and profound stagnation of industry, in order to prove it to one's complete satisfaction. Germany wisely and far-sightedly made a sincere and vigourous effort to comply with the conditions of the treaty; and by so doing she has carried the rest of the world to the verge of economic collapse. The damage wrought by the war was in general of a spectacular and impressive type, and was indeed very great—no one would minimize it—but the damage, present and prospective, wrought by the treaty of peace is much greater and more far-reaching.

The political inheritors of those who made the peace are now extremely uneasy about it. Their predecessors (including Mr. Lloyd George, who still remains in office) had flogged up popular hatred against the Central Empires at such a rate that when they took office they still had, or thought they had, to court and indulge this hatred. Thus we found Mr. Secretary Hughes, for example, in his first communication to the German Government, laying it down that the basis of the Versailles treaty was sound that Germany was solely responsible for the war. He spoke of it quite in the vein of Mr. Lloyd George, as a *chose jugée.* After having promulgated the treaty with such immense ceremony, and raised such preposterous and extravagant popular expectations on the strength of it, the architects of the treaty bequeathed an exceedingly difficult task to their successors; the task of letting the public down, diverting their attention with this or that gesture, taking their mind off their disappointments and scaling down their expectations, so that in time it might be safe to let the Versailles treaty begin to sink out of sight.

The task is being undertaken; the curious piece of mountebankery recently staged in Washington, for example, was an ambitious effort to keep the peoples, particularly those of Europe, hopeful, confiding and diverted; and if economic conditions permit, if times do not become too hard, it may succeed. The politicians can not say outright that the theory of the Versailles treaty is dishonest and outrageous, and that the only chance of peace and well-being is by tearing up the treaty and starting anew on another basis entirely. They can not say this on account of the exigencies of their detestable trade. The best that they can do is what they are doing. They must wait until the state of public feeling permits them to ease down from their uncompromising stand upon the treaty. Gradually, they expect, the public will accustom itself to the idea of relaxations and accommodations, as it sees, from day to day, the patent impracticability of any other course; feelings will weaken, asperities soften, hatreds die out, contacts and approaches of one kind or another will take place; and finally, these public men or their political inheritors will think themselves able to effect in an unobtrusive way, such substantial modifications of the treaty of Versailles as will amount to its annulment.

The process is worth accelerating by every means possible; and what I have here done is meant to assist it. There are many persons in the country who are not politicians, and who are capable and desirous of approaching a matter of this kind with intellectual honesty. Quite possibly they are not aware, many of them, that the Versailles treaty postulates the sole responsibility of the German Government for bringing on the war; undoubtedly they are not acquainted with such evidence as I have here compiled to show that this assumption is unjust and erroneous. Having read this evidence, they will be in a position to review the terms of the Versailles treaty and reassess the justice of those terms. They will also be able to understand the unwillingness, the inability, of the German people to acquiesce in those terms; and they can comprehend the slowness and difficulty wherewith peace and good feeling are being re-established in Europe, and the extreme precariousness and uncertainty of Europe's situation —and our own, in consequence—throughout a future that seems longer than one cares to contemplate.

The reader will perceive at once that this book is a mere compilation and transcription of fact, containing not a shred of opinion or of any original matter. On this account it was published anonymously in its serial form, because it seemed to me that such work should be judged strictly as it stands, without regard to the authority, or lack of authority, which the compiler might happen to possess. Almost all of it is lifted straight from the works of my friends Mr. Francis Neilson and Mr. E. D. Morel. I earnestly hope—indeed, it is my chief motive in publishing this book—that it may serve as an introduction to these words. I can not place too high an estimate upon their importance to a student of British and Continental diplomacy. They are, as far as I know, alone in their field; nothing else can take their place. They are so thorough, so exhaustive and so authoritative that I wonder at their being so little known in the United States. Mr. Morel's works, *Ten Years of Secret Diplomacy*, *Truth and the War*, and *Diplomacy Revealed*, are simply indispensable. Mr. Neilson's book *How Diplomats Make War*, is not an easy book to read; no more are Mr. Morel's; but without having read it no serious student can possibly do justice to the subject.

ALBERT JAY NOCK

THE MYTH OF A GUILTY NATION

I

THE present course of events in Europe is impressing on us once more the truth that military victory, if it is to stand, must also be demonstrably a victory for justice. In the long run, victory must appeal to the sense of justice in the conquered no less than in the conquerors, if it is to be effective. There is no way of getting around this. Mr. Gilbert K. Chesterton is right when he says that if the South had not finally accepted the outcome of the Civil War as being on the whole just, Lincoln would have been wrong in trying to preserve the Union; which is only another way of expressing Lincoln's own homely saying that nothing is ever really settled until it is settled right. The present condition of Europe is largely due to the fact that the official peacemakers have not taken into their reckoning the

German people's sense of justice. Their mistake—it was also Mr. Wilson's great mistake—was in their disregard of what Bismarck called the imponderabilia. The terms of the peace treaty plainly reflect this mistake. That is largely the reason why the treaty is to-day inoperative and worthless. That is largely why the Governments of Europe are confronted with the inescapable alternative: they can either tear up the treaty and replace it by an understanding based on justice, or they can stick to the treaty and by so doing protract indefinitely the dismal succession of wars, revolutions, bankruptcies and commercial dislocations that the treaty inaugurated.

That is the situation; and it is a situation in which the people of the United States have an interest to preserve—the primary interest of a creditor, and also the interest of a trader who needs a large and stable market. It is idle to suppose that American business can prosper so long as Europe remains in a condition of instability and insolvency. Our business is adjusted to the scale of a solvent Europe, and it can not be readjusted without irreparable damage. Until certain matters connected with the war are resolutely put under review, Europe can not be reconstructed, and the United States can not be prosperous. The only thing that can better our own situation is the resumption of normal economic life in Europe; and this can be done only through a thorough reconsideration of the injustices that have been put upon the German people by the conditions of the armistice and the peace treaty.

Of these injustices, the greatest, because it is the foundation for all the rest, is the imputation of Germany's sole responsibility for the war. The German people will never endure that imputation; they should never be expected to endure it. Nothing can really be settled until the question of responsibility is openly and candidly re-examined, and an understanding established that is based on facts instead of on official misrepresentation. This question is by no means one of abstract justice alone, or of chivalry and fair play towards a defeated enemy. It is a question of self-interest, immediate and urgent. However it may be regarded by the American sense of justice and fair play, it remains, to the eye of American industry and commerce, a straight question of dollars and cents. The prosperity of the United States, as we are beginning to see, hangs upon the economic re-establishment of Europe. Europe can not possibly be settled upon the present terms of peace; and these terms can not be changed without first vacating the theory of Germany's sole responsibility, because it is upon this theory that the treaty of Versailles was built. This theory, therefore, must be re-examined in the light of evidence that the Allied and Associated Governments have done their best either to ignore or to suppress. Hence, for the American people, the way to prosperity lies through a searching and honest examination of this theory that has been so deeply implanted in their mind —the theory of a brigand-nation, plotting in solitude to achieve the mastery of the world by fire and sword.

Americans, however, come reluctantly to the task of this examination, for two reasons. First, we are all tired of the war, we hate to think of it or of anything connected with it, and as far as possible, we keep it out of our minds. Second, nearly every reputation of any consequence in this country, political, clerical, academic and journalistic, is already committed, head over ears, to the validity of this theory. How many of our politicians are there whose reputations are not bound up inextricably with this legend of a German plot? How many of our newspaper-editors managed to preserve detachment enough under the pressure of war-propaganda to be able to come forward to-day and say that the question of responsibility for the war should be re-opened? How can the pro-war liberals and ex-pacifists ask for such an inquest when they were all swept off their feet by the specious plea that *this* war was a different war from all other wars in the history of mankind? What can our ministers of religion say after the unreserved endorsement that they put upon the sanctity of the Allied cause? What can our educators say, after having served so zealously the ends of the official propagandists? From our journalists and men of letters what can we expect—after all his rodomontade about Potsdam and the Potsdam gang, how could we expect Dr. Henry Van Dyke, for instance, to face the fact that the portentous Potsdam meeting of the Crown Council on 5 July, 1914, *never took place at all?* There is no use in trying to put a breaking-strain upon human nature, or, on the other hand, in assuming a pharisaic attitude towards its simplest and commonest frailties. It is best, under the circumstances, merely to understand that on this question every institutional voice in the United States is tongue-tied. Press, pulpit, schools and universities, charities and foundations, forums, all are silent; and to expect them to break their silence is to expect more than should be expected from the pride of opinion in average human nature.

II

In examining the evidence let us first take Mr. Lloyd George's own statement of the theory. Except in one particular, it presents the case against Germany quite as it has been rehearsed by nearly every institutional voice in the United States. On 4 August, 1917—after America's entry into the war—the British Premier said:

> What are we fighting for? To defeat the most dangerous conspiracy ever plotted against the liberty of nations; carefully, skilfully, insidiously, clandestinely planned in every detail, with ruthless, cynical determination.

Except for one point, this statement sums up what we have all heard to be the essential doctrine of the war. The one missing point in Mr. Lloyd George's indictment is that the great German conspiracy was launched upon an *unprepared* Europe. In Europe itself, the official propagandists did not make much of this particular point, for far too many people knew better; but in the United States it was promulgated widely. Indeed, this romance of Allied unpreparedness was an essential part of the whole story of German responsibility. Germany, so the official story ran, not only plotted in secret, but she sprung her plot upon a Europe that was wholly unprepared and unsuspecting. Her action was like that of a highwayman leaping from ambush upon a defenceless wayfarer. Belgium was unprepared, France unprepared, Russia unprepared, England unprepared; and in face of an unprovoked attack, these nations hurriedly drew together in an extemporized union, and held the "mad dog" at bay with an extemporized defence until they could devise a plan of common action and a pooling of military and naval resources.

Such, then, is a fair statement of the doctrine of the war as America was taught it. Next, in order to show how fundamental this doctrine is to the terms of the peace treaty, let us consider another statement of Mr. Lloyd George made 3 March, 1921:

> For the allies, German responsibility for the war is fundamental. It is the basis upon which the structure of the treaty of Versailles has been erected, and if that acknowledgment is repudiated or abandoned, the treaty is destroyed. ... We wish, therefore, once and for all, to make it quite clear that German responsibility for the war must be treated by the Allies as a *chose jugée.*

Thus the British Premier explicitly declares that the treaty of Versailles is based upon the theory of Germany's sole responsibility.

Now, as against this theory, the main facts may be summarized as follows: (1) The British and French General Staffs had been in active collaboration for war with Germany ever since January 1906. (2) The British and French Admiralty had been in similar collaboration. (3) The late Lord Fisher [First Sea Lord of the British Admiralty], twice in the course of these preparations, proposed an attack upon the German fleet and a landing upon the coast of Pomerania, *without a declaration of war.* (4) Russia had been preparing for war ever since 1909, and the Russian and French General Staffs had come to a formal understanding that Russian mobilization should be held equivalent to a declaration of war. (5) Russian mobilization was begun in the spring of 1914, under the guise of "tests," and these tests were carried on continuously to the outbreak of the war. (6) In April, 1914, four months before the war, the Russian and French naval authorities initiated joint plans for maritime operations against Germany. (7) Up to the outbreak of the war, Germany was selling grain in considerable quantities to both France and Russia. (8) It can not be shown that the German

Government ever in a single instance, throughout all its dealings with foreign Governments, demanded or intimated for Germany anything more than a position of economic equality with other nations.

These facts, among others to which reference will hereafter be made, have come to light only since the outbreak of the war. They effectively dispose of the theory of an unprepared and unsuspecting Europe; and a historical survey of them excludes absolutely, and stamps as utterly untenable and preposterous, the theory of a deliberate German plot against the peace of the world.

III

Let us now consider the idea so generally held in America, though not in Europe, that in 1914, England and the Continental nations were not expecting war and not prepared for war. The fact is that Europe was as thoroughly organized for war as it could possibly be. The point to which that organization was carried by England, France and Russia, as compared with Germany and Austria, may to some extent be indicated by statistics. In 1913, Russia carried a military establishment (on a peace footing) of 1,284,000 men; France, by an addition of 183,000 men, proposed to raise her peace-establishment to a total of 741,572. Germany, by an addition of 174,373 men, proposed to raise her total to 821,964; and Austria, by additions of 58,505 already made, brought her total up to 473,643. These are the figures of the British War Office, as furnished to the House of Commons in 1913.

Here is a set of figures that is even more interesting and significant. From 1909 to 1914, the amount spent on new naval construction by England, France and Russia, as compared with Germany, was as follows:

	England	France	Russia	Germany
1909	£11,076,551	£ 4,517,766	£ 1,758,487	£10,177,062
1910	£14,755,289	£ 4,977,682	£ 1,424,013	£11,392,856
1911	£15,148,171	£ 5,876,659	£ 3,216,396	£11,710,859
1912	£16,132,558	£ 7,114,876	£ 6,897,580	£11,491,187
1913	£16,883,875	£ 8,893,064	£12,082,516	£11,010,883
1914	£18,676,080	£11,772,862	£13,098,613	£10,316,264

These figures can not be too carefully studied by those who have been led to think that Germany pounced upon a defenceless and unsuspecting Europe like a cat upon a mouse. If it be thought worth while to consider also the period of a few years preceding 1909, one finds that England's superiority in battleships alone was 112 per cent in 1901, and her superiority rose to nearly 200 per cent in 1904; in which year England spent £42,431,000 on her navy, and Germany £11,659,000. Taking the comparative statistics of naval expenditure from 1900, in which year England spent £32,055,000 on her navy, and Germany spent £7,472,000, down to 1914 it is absolutely impossible to make the figures show that Germany enforced upon the other nations of Europe an unwilling competition in naval armament.

But the German army! According to all accounts of German militarism which were suffered to reach these shores, it is here that we shall find evidence of what Mr. Lloyd George, on 4 August, 1917, called "the most dangerous conspiracy ever plotted against the liberty of nations; carefully, skilfully, insidiously, clandestinely planned in every detail, with ruthless, cynical determination." Well, if one chooses to hold the current view of German militarism, it must be admitted that Germany had at her disposal some miraculous means of getting something for nothing, getting a great deal for nothing, in fact, for on any other supposition, the figures are far from supporting that view. In 1914 (pre-war figures), Germany and Austria together carried an army-expenditure of £92 million; England, France and Russia together carried one of £142 million. England "had no army," it was said; all her military strength lay in her navy. If that were true, then it must be said that she had as miraculous a faculty as Germany's; only, whereas Germany's was a faculty for getting more than her money's worth, England's was for getting less than her money's worth. England's army-expenditure for 1914 (pre-war figures) was £28 million; £4 million more than Austria's. Nor was this a sudden emergency-outlay. Going back as far as 1905, we find that she laid out in that year the same amount, £28 million. In that year, Germany and Austria together spent £48 million on their armies; England, France and Russia together spent £94 million on theirs. If between 1905 and 1913, England, France and Russia spent any such sums upon their armies as their statistics show, and nothing came of it but an unprepared and unsuspecting Europe in 1914, it seems clear that the taxpayers of those countries were swindled on an inconceivably large scale.

IV

At this point, some questions may be raised. Why, in the decade preceding 1914, did England, France and Russia arm themselves at the rate indicated by the foregoing figures? Why did they accelerate their naval development progressively from about £17 million in 1909 to about £43 million in 1914? Why did Russia alone propose to raise her military peace-establishment to an army of 1,700,000, more than double the size of Germany's army? Against whom were these preparations directed, and understood to be directed? Certainly not against one another. France and Russia had been bound by a military convention ever since 17 August, 1892; England and France had been bound since January, 1906, by a similar pact; and this was subsequently extended to include Belgium. These agreements will be considered in detail hereafter; they are now mentioned merely to show that the military activity in these countries was not independent in purpose. France, England, Russia and Belgium were not uneasy about one another and not arming against one another; nor is there any evidence that anyone thought that they were. It was against the Central Empires only that these preparations were addressed. Nor can one who scans the table of relative expenditure easily believe that the English–French–Russian combination was effected for purely defensive purposes; and taking the diplomatic history of the period in conjunction with the testimony of the budgets, such belief becomes impossible.

V

The British Government is the one which was most often represented to us as taken utterly by surprise by the German onslaught on Belgium. Let us see. The Austrian Archduke was assassinated 28 June, 1914, by three men who, according to wide report in Europe and absolute certainty in America, were secret agents of the German Government, acting under German official instruction. The findings of the court of inquiry showed that they were Serbs, members of a pan-Slav organization; that the assassination was plotted in Belgrade, and the weapons with which it was committed were obtained there.[1] Serbia denied all connexion with the assassins (the policy of Serbia being then controlled by the Russian Foreign Office), and then the Russian Government stepped forward to prevent the

[1]Six months after the armistice, the bodies of the three assassins were dug up, according to a Central News dispatch from Prague, "with great solemnity, in the presence of thousands of the inhabitants. The remains of *these Serbian officers* are to be sent to their native country." This is a naïve statement. It remains to be explained why these "German agents" should be honoured in this distinguished way by the Serbs!

humiliation of Serbia by Austria. It is clear from the published diplomatic documents that the British Foreign Office knew everything that took place between the assassination and the burial of the Archduke; all the facts, that is, connected with the murder. The first dispatch in the British White Paper is dated 20 July, and it is addressed to the British Ambassador at Berlin. One wonders why not to the Ambassador at Vienna; also one wonders why the diplomats apparently found nothing to write about for nearly three weeks between the Archduke's funeral and 20 July. It is a strange silence. Sir Edward Grey, however, made a statement in the House of Commons, 27 July, in which he gave the impression that he got his first information about the course of the quarrel between Austria and Serbia no earlier than 24 July, three days before. The Ambassador at Vienna, Sir M. de Bunsen, had, notwithstanding, telegraphed him that the Austrian Premier had given him no hint of "the impending storm" and that it was from a private source "that I received, 15 July, the forecast of what was about to happen, concerning which I *telegraphed to you the following day*." Sir Maurice de Bunsen's telegram on this important subject thus evidently was suppressed; and the only obvious reason for the suppression is that it carried evidence that Sir E. Grey was thoroughly well posted by 16 July on what was taking place in Vienna. Sir M. de Bunsen's allusion to this telegram confirms this assumption; in fact, it can be interpreted in no other way.

On 28 July, the House of Commons was informed that Austria had declared war on Serbia. Two days later, 30 July, Sir E. Grey added the item of information that Russia had ordered a partial mobilization "which has not hitherto led to any corresponding steps by other Powers, so far as our information goes." Sir E. Grey did not add, however, that he knew quite well what "corresponding steps" other Powers were likely to take. He knew the terms of the Russian–French military convention, under which a mobilization by Russia was to be held equivalent to a declaration of war; he also knew the terms of the English–French agreement which he himself had authorized—although up to the eve of the war he denied, in reply to questions in the House of Commons, that any such agreement existed, and acknowledged it only on 3 August, 1914.[2] He had promised Sazonov, the Russian Foreign Minister, in 1912, that in the event of Germany's coming to Austria's aid, Russia could rely on Great Britain to "stake everything in order to inflict the most serious blow to German

[2]See footnote to chapter XVIII

power." To say that Sir E. Grey, and *à fortiori* Mr. Asquith, the Prime Minister; Lord Haldane, the Minister for War, whose own book has been a most tremendous let-down to the fictions of the propagandists; Mr. Winston Churchill, head of the Admiralty, who at Dundee, 5 June, 1915, declared that he had been sent to the Admiralty in 1911 with the express duty laid upon him by the Prime Minister to put the fleet in a state of instant and constant readiness for war; to say that these men were taken by surprise and unprepared, is mere levity.

Austria was supposed to be, and still is by some believed to have been, Germany's vassal State, and by menacing Serbia to have been doing Germany's dirty work. No evidence of this has been adduced; and the trouble with this idea of Austria's status is that it breaks down before the report of Sir M. de Bunsen, 1 September, 1914, that Austria finally yielded and agreed to accept all the proposals of the Powers for mediation between herself and Serbia. She made every concession. Russian mobilization, however, had begun on 25 July and become general four days later; and it was not stopped. Germany then gave notice that she would mobilize her army if Russian mobilization was not stopped in twelve hours; and also, knowing the terms of the Russian–French convention of 1892, she served notice on France, giving her eighteen hours to declare her position. Russia made no reply; France answered that she would do what she thought best in her own interest; and almost at the moment, on 1 August, when Germany ordered a general mobilization, Russian troops were over her border, the British fleet had been mobilized for a week in the North Sea, and British merchant ships were lying at Kronstadt, empty, to convey Russian troops from that port to the Pomeranian coast, in pursuance of the plan indicated by Lord Fisher in his autobiography, recently published. These matters are well summed up by Lord Loreburn, as follows:

> Serbia gave offence to the Austro-Hungarian Empire, cause of just offence, as our Ambassador frankly admits in his published dispatches. We [England] had no concern in that quarrel, as Sir Edward Grey says in terms. But Russia, the protectress of Serbia, came forward to prevent her being utterly humiliated by Austria. We were not concerned in that quarrel either, as Sir Edward also says. And then Russia called upon France under their treaty to help in the fight. France was not concerned in that quarrel any more than ourselves, as Sir Edward informs us. But France was bound by a Russian treaty, of which he did not know the terms, and then France called on us for help. We were tied

by the relations which our Foreign Office had created, without apparently realizing that they had created them.

In saying that Sir E. Grey did not know the terms of the Franco-Russian agreement, Lord Loreburn is generous, probably more generous than he should be; but that is no matter. The thing to be remarked is that Lord Loreburn's summing-up comes to something wholly different from Mr. Lloyd George's "most dangerous conspiracy ever plotted against the liberty of nations." It comes to something wholly different from the notion implanted in Americans, of Germany pouncing upon a peaceful, unprepared and unsuspecting Europe. The German nation, we may be sure, is keenly aware of this difference; and therefore, any peace which, like the peace of Versailles, is bottomed on the *chose jugée* of laying the sole responsibility for the war at the door of the German nation, or even at the door of the German Government, is simply impracticable and impossible.

VI

If the theory upon which the treaty of Versailles is based, the theory of a single guilty nation, were true, there would be no trouble about saying what the war was fought for. The Allied belligerents would have a simple, straight story to tell; they could describe their aims and intentions clearly in a few words that any one could understand, and their story would be reasonably consistent and not vary greatly from year to year. It would be practically the same story in 1918 as in 1915 or at any time between. In America, indeed, the story did not greatly vary up to the spring of 1917, for the reason that this country was pretty much in the dark about European international relations. Once our indignation and sympathies were aroused, it was for the propagandists mostly a matter of keeping them as hot as possible. Few had the information necessary to discount the plain, easy, understandable story of a robber nation leaping upon an unprepared and defenceless Europe for no cause whatever except the lofty ambition, as Mr. Joseph Choate said, "to establish a world-empire upon the ruins of the British Empire." Those who had this information could not make themselves heard; and thus it was that the propagandists had no need to vary the one story that was most useful to their purpose of keeping us in a state of unreasoning indignation, and accordingly they did not vary it.

In Europe and in England, however, the case was different. International relations were better understood by those who were closer to them than we were; more questions were raised and more demands made. Hence the Allied politicians and propagandists were kept busy upon the defensive. When from time to time the voice of popular discontent or of some influential body of opinion insisted on a statement of the causes of the war or of the war-aims of the Allies, they were confronted with the politician's traditional difficulty. They had to say something plausible and satisfactory, which yet must be something that effectively hid the truth of the situation. As the war hung on, their difficulty became desperate and they threw consistency to the winds, telling any sort of story that would enable them for the moment to "get by." The publication of the secret treaties which had been seined out of the quagmire of the old Russian Foreign Office by the revolutionists made no end of trouble for them. It is amusing now to remember how promptly these treaties were branded by the British Foreign Office as forgeries; especially when it turned out that the actual terms of the armistice not the nominal terms, which were those of Mr. Wilson's Fourteen Points, but the actual terms were the terms of the secret treaties! The publication of the secret treaties in this country did not contribute much towards a disillusionment of the public; the press as a rule ignored or lied about them, they were not widely read, and few who did read them had enough understanding of European affairs to interpret them. But abroad they put a good deal of fat into the fire; and this was a specimen of the kind of thing that the Allied politicians had to contend with in their efforts to keep their peoples in line.

The consequence was that the official and semi-official statements of the causes of the war and of the war-aims of the Allies are a most curious hotchpotch. In fact, if any one takes stock in the theory of the one guilty nation and is therefore convinced that the treaty of Versailles is just and proper and likely to enforce an enduring peace, one could suggest nothing better than that he should go through the literature of the war, pick out these statements, put them in parallel columns, and see how they look. If the war originated in the unwarranted conspiracy of a robber nation, if the aims of the

Allies were to defeat that conspiracy and render it impotent and to chastise and tie the hands of the robber nation—and that is the theory of the treaty of Versailles—can anyone in his right mind suppose that the Allied politicians and propagandists would ever give out, or need to give out, these ludicrously contradictory and inconsistent explanations and statements? When one has a simple, straight story to tell, and a most effective story, why complicate it and undermine it and throw all sorts of doubts upon it, by venturing upon all sorts of public utterances that will not square with it in any conceivable way? Politicians, of all men, never lie for the fun of it; their available margin of truth is always so narrow that they keep within it when they can. Mr. Lloyd George, for example, is one of the cleverest of politicians. We have already considered his two statements; first, that of 4 August, 1917:

> What are we fighting for? To defeat the most dangerous conspiracy ever plotted against the liberty of nations; carefully, skilfully, insidiously, clandestinely planned in every detail with ruthless, cynical determination.

—and then that of 3 March, 1921:

> For the Allies, German responsibility for the war is fundamental. It is the basis upon which

> the structure of the treaty of Versailles has been erected, and if that acknowledgment is repudiated or abandoned, the treaty is destroyed. ...German responsibility for the war must be treated by the Allies as a *chose jugée*.

A little over two months before Mr. George made this latter utterance, on 23 December, 1920, he said this:

> The more one reads memoirs and books written in the various countries of what happened before the first of August, 1914, the more one realizes that no one at the head of affairs quite meant war at that stage. It was something into which they glided, or rather staggered and stumbled, perhaps through folly; and a discussion, I have no doubt, would have averted it.

Well, it would strike an unprejudiced person that if this were true, there is a great deal of doubt put upon Mr. Lloyd George's former statements by Mr. Lloyd George himself. Persons who plot carefully, skilfully, insidiously and clandestinely, do not glide; they do not stagger or stumble, especially through folly. They keep going, as we in America were assured that the German Government did keep going, right up to The Day of their own choosing. Moreover, they are not likely to be headed off by discussion; highwaymen are notoriously curt in their speech and if one attempts discussion with them they become irritable and peremptory. This is the invariable habit of highwaymen. Besides, if discussion would have averted war in 1914, why was it not forthcoming? Certainly not through any fault of the Austrian Government, which made every concession, as the British Ambassador's report shows, notwithstanding its grievance against Serbia was a just one. Certainly not through any fault of the German Government, which never refused discussion and held its hand with all the restraint possible under the circumstances just described. Well, then, how is it so clear that German responsibility for the war should be treated as a *chose jugée*?

VII

People who have a clear and simple case do not talk in this fashion. Picking now at random among the utterances of politicians and propagandists, we find an assorted job-lot of aims assigned and causes alleged, and in all of them there is that curious, incomprehensible and callous disregard of the power of conviction that a straight story always exercises, if you have one to tell. In November, 1917, when the Foreign Office was being pestered by demands for a statement of the Allied war-aims, Lord Robert Cecil said in the House of Commons, that the restitution of Alsace and Lorraine to France was a "well-understood war-aim from the moment we entered the war." As things have turned out, it is an odd coincidence how so many of these places that have iron or coal or oil in them seem to represent a well-understood war-aim. Less than a month before, in October, 1917, General Smuts said that to his mind the one great dominating war-aim was "the end of militarism, the end of standing armies." Well, the Allies won the war, but judging by results, this dominating war-aim seems rather to have been lost sight of. Mr. Lloyd George again on another occasion, said in the House of

Commons that "self-determination was one of the principles for which we entered the war … a principle from which we have never departed since the beginning of the war." This, too, seems an aim that for some reason the victorious nations have not quite realized; indeed in some cases, as in Ireland, for example, there has been no great alacrity shown about trying to realize it. Viscount Bryce said that the war sprang from the strife of races and religions in the Balkan countries, and from the violence done to the sentiment of nationality in Alsace-Lorraine which made France the ally of Russia. But the fact is that France became the ally of Russia on the basis of hard cash, and since the Russian Revolution, she has been a bit out of luck by way of getting her money back. Mr. Asquith in the House of Commons, 3 August, 1914 said:

> If I am asked what we are fighting for, I reply in two sentences. In the first place, to fulfil a solemn international obligation.… Secondly we are fighting … to vindicate the principle that small nationalities are not to be crushed in defiance of international good faith.

Just so: and in the House of Commons, 20 December, 1917, he said:

> The League of Nations … was the avowed purpose, the very purpose … for which we entered

the war and for which we are continuing the war.

You pays your money, you see, and takes your choice. The point to be made, however, is that one who has a strong case, a real case, never trifles with it in this way. Would the reader do it?

VIII

Mr. Asquith's citation of a "solemn international obligation" refers to the so-called Belgian treaties. It will be remembered that the case of Belgium was the great winning card played by the Allied Governments for the stakes of American sympathies; and therefore we may here properly make a survey, somewhat in detail, of the status of Belgium at the outset of the war.

Belgium had learned forty years ago how she stood under the treaties of 1831 and 1839. When in the late 'eighties there was likelihood of a Franco-German war, the question of England's participation under these treaties was thoroughly discussed, and it was shown conclusively that England was not obligated. Perhaps the best summary of the case was that given by Mr. W. T. Stead in the *Pall Mall Gazette* in the issues of 4 and 5 February, 1887. After an examination of the treaties of 1831, 1839 and 1870—an examination unfortunately too long to be quoted here—Mr. Stead briefly sums up the result of his investigation in the following statement:

> There is therefore no English guarantee to Belgium. It is possible perhaps, to 'construct' such

> a guarantee; but the case may be summed up as follows: (1) England is under no guarantee whatever except such as is common to Austria, France, Russia and Germany; (2) that guarantee is not specifically of the neutrality of Belgium at all; and (3) is given, not to Belgium but to the Netherlands.

This was the official view of the British Government at the time, and it is reflected in the celebrated letter signed "Diplomaticus" in the *Standard* of 4 February, to which Mr. Stead refers; which, indeed, he makes the guiding text for his examination. The *Standard* was then the organ of Lord Salisbury's Government, and it is as nearly certain as anything of the sort can be, that the letter signed "Diplomaticus" was written by the hand of the British Prime Minister, Lord Salisbury himself.

How Mr. Asquith's Government in August 1914 came suddenly to extemporize a wholly different view of England's obligations to Belgium is excellently told by that inveterate diarist and chronicler, Mr. Wilfred Scawen Blunt:

> The obligation of fighting in alliance with France in case of a war with Germany concerned the honour of three members only of Asquith's Cabinet, who alone were aware of

the exact promises that had been made. These, though given verbally and with reservations as to the consent of Parliament, bound the three as a matter of personal honour, and were understood at the Quai d'Orsay as binding the British nation. Neither Asquith nor his two companions[1] in this inner Cabinet could have retained office had they gone back from their word in spirit or in letter. It would also doubtless have entailed a serious quarrel with the French Government had they failed to make it good. So clearly was the promise understood at Paris to be binding that President Poincaré, when the crisis came, had written to King George reminding him of it as an engagement made between the two nations which he counted on His Majesty to keep.

Thus faced, the case was laid before the Cabinet, but was found to fail as a convincing argument for war. It was then that Asquith, with his lawyer's instinct, at a second Cabinet meeting brought forward the neutrality of Belgium as a better plea than the other to lay before a British jury, and by representing the neutrality-treaties of 1831 and 1839 as entailing an obligation on England to fight (of which the text of the treaties contains no word) obtained the Cabinet's consent, and war was declared.

[1] Sir E. Grey and Lord Haldane.

Belgium was not thought of by the British Cabinet before 2 August, 1914. She was brought in then as a means of making the war go down with the British people. The fact is that Belgium was thoroughly prepared for war, thoroughly prepared for just what happened to her. Belgium was a party to the military arrangements effected among France, England and Russia; for this we have the testimony of Marshal Joffre before the Metallurgic Committee in Paris, and also the record of the "conversations" that were carried on in Brussels between the Belgian chief of staff and Lt.-Col. Barnardiston. On 24 July, 1914, the day when the Austrian note was presented to Serbia (the note of which Sir E. Grey had gotten an intimation as early as 16 July by telegraph from the British Ambassador at Vienna, Sir M. de Bunsen), the Belgian Foreign Minister, M. Davignon, promptly dispatched to all the Belgian embassies an identical communication containing the following statement, the significance of which is made clear by a glance at a map:

> All necessary steps to ensure respect of Belgian neutrality have nevertheless been taken by the Government. The Belgian army has been mobilized and is taking up such strategic positions as have been chosen to secure the defence of the country and the respect of its neutrality.

> The forts of Antwerp and on the Meuse have been put in a state of defence.

It was on the eastern frontier, we perceive, therefore—not on the western, where Belgium might have been invaded by France—that all the available Belgian military force was concentrated. Hence, to pretend any longer that the Belgian Government was surprised by the action of Germany, or unprepared to meet it; to picture Germany and Belgium as cat and mouse, to understand the position of Belgium otherwise than that she was one of four solid allies under definite agreement worked out in complete practical detail, is sheer absurdity.

IX

If the official theory of German responsibility were correct, it would be impossible to explain the German Government's choice of the year 1914 as a time to strike at "an unsuspecting and defenceless Europe." The figures quoted in Chapter III show that the military strength of Germany, relatively to that of the French–Russian–English combination, had been decreasing since 1910. If Germany had wished to strike at Europe, she had two first-rate chances, one in 1908 and another in 1912, and not only let them both go by, but threw all her weight on the side of peace. This is inexplicable upon the theory that animates the treaty of Versailles. Germany was then in a position of advantage. The occasion presented itself in 1908, in Serbia's quarrel with Austria over the annexation of Bosnia and the Herzegovina. Russia, which was backing Serbia, was in no shape to fight; her military strength, used up in the Russo-Japanese war, had not recovered. France would not at this time have been willing to go to war with Germany over her weak ally's commitments in the Danube States. Germany, however, contented herself with serving notice on the Tsar of her unequivocal support of Austria; and this was enough. The Tsar accepted the *fait accompli* of the annexation of Bosnia and the Herzegovina; Serbia retired and cooled off; and Turkey, from whom the annexed province was ravished, was compensated by Austria. It is not to the point to scrutinize the propriety of these transactions; the point is that Germany held the peace of Europe in the hollow of her hand, with immense advantages in her favour, and chose not to close her hand. The comment of a neutral diplomat, the Belgian Minister in Berlin, is interesting. In his report of 1 April, 1909, to the Belgian Foreign Office, he says:

> The conference scheme elaborated by M. Isvolsky and Sir Edward Grey; the negotiations for collective representations in Vienna; and the whole exchange of ideas among London, Paris and Petersburg, were steadily aimed at forcing Austria-Hungary into a transaction which would strongly have resembled a humiliation. This humiliation would have affected Germany as directly and as sensibly as Austria-Hungary, and would have struck a heavy blow at the confidence which is inspired in Vienna by the alliance with Germany. These machinations were frustrated by Germany's absolutely unequivocal and decided attitude, from which she has never departed in spite of all the urgings with which she has been harassed. Germany alone

> has accomplished the preservation of peace. The new grouping of the Powers, organized by the King of England, has measured its forces with the alliance of the Central European Powers, and has shown itself incapable of impairing the same. Hence the vexation which is manifested.

The last two sentences of the foregoing seem to show—putting it mildly—that the Belgian Minister did not suspect the German Government of any aggressive spirit. In the same dispatch, moreover, he remarks:

> As always, when everything does not go as the French, English or Russian politicians want it to, the *Temps* shows its bad temper. Germany is the scapegoat.

Again, at the time of the Balkan War in 1912, Germany had an excellent opportunity to gratify her military ambition, if she had any, at the expense of an "unsuspecting and unprepared Europe"; not as advantageous as in 1908 but more advantageous than in 1914. Serbia's provocations against Austria-Hungary had become so great that the Austrian Archduke (assassinated in 1914 at Sarajevo) told the German Emperor personally that they had reached the limit of endurance. On this occasion also, however, William II put himself definitely on the side of peace, and in so doing left the Austrian Government somewhat disappointed and discontented. Another neutral diplomat reports of the German Foreign Minister that

> whatever plans he may have in his head (and he has big ideas), for winning the sympathies of the young Balkan Powers over to Germany, one thing is absolutely certain, and that is that he is rigidly determined to avoid a European conflagration. On this point the policy of Germany is similar to that of England and France, both of which countries are determinedly pacifist.

This is a fair statement of the English and French position in 1912. There was a great revulsion of feeling in England after her close shave of being dragged into war over Morocco and her sentiment was all for attending to certain pressing, domestic problems. Besides, it was only in November, 1911, and only through the indiscretion of a French newspaper, that the British public (and the British Parliament as well) had learned that the Anglo-French agreement of 1904 had secret articles attached to it, out of which had emanated the imbroglio over Morocco; and there was a considerable feeling of distrust towards the Foreign Office. In fact, Sir E. Grey, the Foreign Minister, was so unpopular with his own party that quite probably he would have had to get out of office if he had not been sustained by Tory influence. Mr. W. T. Stead expressed a quite general sentiment in the *Review of Reviews* for December, 1911:

> The fact remains that in order to put France in possession of Morocco, we all but went to war with Germany. We have escaped war, but we have not escaped the national and abiding enmity of the German people. Is it possible to frame a heavier indictment of the foreign policy of any British Ministry? The secret, the open secret, of this almost incredible crime against treaty-faith, British interests and the peace of the world, is the unfortunate fact that Sir Edward Grey has been dominated by men in the Foreign Office who believe all considerations must be subordinated to the one supreme duty of thwarting Germany at every turn, even if in doing so British interests, treaty-faith and the peace of the world are trampled underfoot. I speak that of which I know.

This was strong language and it went without challenge, for too many Englishmen felt that way. In France, the Poincaré–Millerand–Delcassé combination was getting well into the saddle; but with English public opinion in this notably undependable condition, English support of France, in spite of the secret agreement binding the two governments, was decidedly risky. Thereupon France also was "determinedly pacifist." Now if Germany had been the prime mover in "the most dangerous conspiracy ever plotted against the liberty of nations," why did she not take advantage of that situation?

Russia, too, was "determinedly pacifist" in 1912, and with good reason. There was a party of considerable influence in the Tsar's court that was strongly for going to war in behalf of Serbia, but it was finally headed off by the Foreign Minister, Sazonov, who knew the state of public opinion in England and its effect on France, and knew therefore that the French–Russian–English alliance was not yet in shape to take on large orders. It is true that the Poincaré–Millerand–Delcassé war-party in France had proof enough in 1912 that it could count on the British Government's support; and what France knew, Russia knew. Undoubtedly, too, the British Government would somehow, under some pretext or other, possibly Belgian neutrality, have contrived to redeem its obligations as it did in 1914. But the atmosphere of the country was not favourable and the thing would have been difficult. Accordingly, Sazonov saw that it was best for him to restrain Serbia's impetuosity and truculence for the time being—Russia herself being none too ready—and accordingly he did so.

But how? The Serbian Minister at Petersburg says that Sazonov told him that in view of Serbia's successes "he had confidence in our strength and believed that we would be able to deliver a blow at Austria. For that reason we should feel satisfied with what we were to receive, and consider it merely as a temporary halting-place on the road to further gains." On another occasion "Sazonov told me that we must work for the future because we would acquire a great deal of territory from Austria." The Serbian Minister at Bucharest says that his Russian and French colleagues counselled a policy of waiting "with as great a degree of preparedness as possible the important events which must make their appearance among the Great Powers." How, one may ask, was the Russian Foreign Office able to look so far and so clearly into the future? If German responsibility for the war is fundamental, a *chose jugée*, as Mr. Lloyd George said it is, this seems a strange way for the Russian Foreign Minister to be talking, as far back as 1912. But stranger still is the fact that the German Government did not jump in at this juncture instead of postponing its blow until 1914 when every one was apparently quite ready to receive it. When the historian of the future considers the theory of the Versailles treaty and considers the behaviour of the German Government in the crisis of 1908 and in the crisis of 1912, he will have to scratch his head a great deal to make them harmonize.

X

By the spring of 1913, the diplomatic representatives of the Allied Danube States made no secret of the relations in which their Governments stood to the Tsar's Foreign Office. The Balkan League was put through by Russian influence and Russia controlled its diplomacy. Serbia was as completely the instrument of Russia as Poland is now the instrument of France. "If the Austrian troops invade Balkan territory," wrote Baron Beyens on 4 April, 1913, "it would give cause for Russia to intervene, and might let loose a universal war." Now, if Germany had been plotting "with ruthless, cynical determination," as Mr. Lloyd George said, against the peace of Europe, what inconceivable stupidity for her not to push Austria along rather than do everything possible to hold her back! Why give Russia the benefit of eighteen months of valuable time for the feverish campaign of "preparedness" that she carried on? Those eighteen months meant a great deal. In February, 1914, the Tsar arranged to provide the Serbian army with rifles and artillery, Serbia agreeing to put half a million soldiers in the field. In the same month Russia negotiated a French loan of about $100 million for improvements on her strategic railways and frontier-roads. During the spring, she made "test" mobilizations of large bodies of troops which were never demobilized, and these "test" mobilizations continued down to the outbreak of the war; and in April Russian agents made technical arrangements with agents of the British and French Admiralties for possible combined naval action.

Yes, those eighteen months were very busy months for Russia. True, she came out at the end of them an "unprepared and unsuspecting" nation, presumably, for was not all Europe unprepared and unsuspecting? Is it not so nominated in the Versailles treaty? One can not help wondering, however, how it is that Germany, "carefully, skilfully, insidiously, clandestinely planning in every detail" a murderous attack on the peace of Europe, should have given Russia the inestimable advantage of those eighteen months.

XI

Mr. E. D. Morel, editor of the British monthly *Foreign Affairs*, performed more than a distinguished service—it is a splendid, an illustrious service—to the disparaged cause of justice, when recently he translated and published in England through the National Labour Press, a series of remarkable State documents.[1] This consists of reports made by the Belgian diplomatic representatives at Paris, London and Berlin, to the Belgian Minister of Foreign Affairs, covering the period from 7 February, 1905 to 2 July, 1914. Their authenticity has never been questioned. They have received no notice in this country; their content and import were carefully kept from the American people as long as it was possible to do so, and consequently they remain unknown except to a few who are students of international affairs or who have some similar special interest.

It can hardly be pretended by anyone that Belgian officials had, during that decade, any particular love or leaning towards Germany. The Belgian Foreign Office has always been as free from sentimental attachments as any other. It has always been governed by the same

[1]Under the title *Diplomacy Revealed.*

motives that govern the British, French, German and Russian Foreign Offices. Its number, like theirs, was number one; it was out, first and last, for the interests of the Belgian Government, and it scrutinized every international transaction from the viewpoint of those interests and those only. It was fully aware of the position of Belgium as a mere "strategic corridor" and battle-ground for alien armies in case of a general European war, and aware that Belgium had simply to make the best of its bad outlook, for nothing else could be done. If the Belgian Foreign Office and its agents, moreover, had no special love for Germany, neither had they any special fear of her. They were in no more or deeper dread of a German invasion than of a British or French invasion. In fact, in 1911, the Belgian Minister at Berlin set forth in a most matter-of-fact way his belief that in the event of war, Belgian neutrality would be first violated by Great Britain.[2] These observers, in short,

[2]This belief received some corroboration in the spring of 1912, when in the course of military "conversations," the British Military Attaché, Lieutenant-Colonel Bridges, told the Belgian Minister of War that if war had broken out over the Agadir incident in 1911, the British Government would have landed troops in Belgium with or without the Belgian Government's consent. So much did the British Government think of the "scrap of paper!"

may on all accounts, as far as one can see, be accepted as neutral and disinterested, with the peculiar disinterestedness of one who has no choice between two evils.

Well, then, under the circumstances it is remarkable that if Germany during the ten years preceding August, 1914, were plotting against the peace of the world, these Belgian observers seem unaware of it. It is equally noteworthy that if Germany's assault were unprovoked, they seem unaware of that also. These documents relate in an extremely matter-of-fact way a continuous series of extraordinary provocations put upon the German Government, and moreover, they represent the behaviour of the German Government, under these provocations, in a very favourable light. On the other hand, they show from beginning to end a most profound distrust of English diplomacy. If there is any uncertainty about the causes of ill-feeling between England and Germany, these Belgian officials certainly do not share it. They regularly speak of England's jealousy of Germany's economic competition, and the provocative attitude to which this jealousy gave rise. They speak of it, moreover, as though it were something that the Belgian Government were already well aware of; they speak of it in the tone of pure commonplace, such as one might use in an incidental reference to the weather or to a tariff-schedule or to any other matter that is well understood and about which there is no difference of opinion and nothing new to be said. This is all the more remarkable in view of the fact that it was nominally to save Belgium and to defend the sanctity of Belgian neutrality that England entered the war in August, 1914. These Belgian agents are invariably suspicious of English diplomacy, as Mr. E. D. Morel points out, "mainly because they feel that it is tending to make the war which they dread for their country." They persistently and unanimously "insinuate that if left to themselves, France and Germany would reach a settlement of their differences, and that British diplomacy was being continually exercised to envenom the controversy and to draw a circle of hostile alliances round Germany." This, indeed, under a specious concern for the "balance of power," has been the historic rôle of English diplomacy. Every one remembers how in 1866, just before the Franco-Prussian war, Mr. Matthew Arnold's imaginary Prussian, Arminius von Thunder-ten-Tronckh, wrote to the editor of the *Pall Mall Gazette*, begging him to prevail upon his fellow-countrymen "for Heaven's sake not to go on biting, first the French Emperor's tail, and then ours."

On 18 February, 1905, the Belgian Minister in Berlin reported thus:

> The real cause of the English hatred of Germany is the jealousy aroused by the astonishing development of Germany's merchant navy and of her commerce and manufactures. This hatred will last until the English have thoroughly learned to understand that the world's trade is not by rights an exclusively English monopoly. Moreover, it is studiously fostered by the *Times* and a whole string of other daily papers and periodicals that do not stop short of calumny in order to pander to the tastes of their readers.

At that time the centre of the English navy had just been shifted to the North Sea, to the accompaniment of a very disturbing and, as at first reported, a very flamboyant speech from the Civil Lord of the Admiralty, Mr. Lee. Of the sensation thereby created in Germany, the Belgian Minister says:

> In informing the British public that Germany does not dream of any aggression against England, Count Bülow [the German Chancellor] said no more than what is recognized by every one who considers the matter dispassionately. Germany would have nothing to gain from a contest.... The German fleet has been created with a purely defensive object: The small capacity of the coal-bunkers in her High Seas Fleet,

and the small number of her cruisers, prove besides that her fleet is not intended for use at any distance from the coast.

On the other hand, he remarks in the same report:

> It was obvious that the new disposition of the English navy was aimed at Germany … it certainly is not because of Russia, whose material stock is to a great extent destroyed and whose navy has just given striking proof of incompetence [in the Russo-Japanese war].

Such is the tone uniformly adopted by these neutral observers throughout their reports from 1905 to 1914. On 24 October, 1905, the Belgian Minister in Paris wrote:

> England, in her efforts to maintain her supremacy and to hinder the development of her great German rival, is evidently inspired by the wish to avoid a conflict, but are not her selfish aims in themselves bringing it upon us?… She thought, when she concluded the Japanese alliance and gradually drew France into similar ties, that she had found the means to her end, by sufficiently paralysing Germany's powers as to make war impossible.

This view of the Anglo-Japanese alliance is interesting and significant, especially now when that instrument is coming up for renewal, with the United States standing towards England in the same relation of economic competitorship that Germany occupied in 1905. True, Viscount Bryce assured the Institute of Politics at Williams College last summer that it was not Germany's economic rivalry that disturbed England; but on this point it would be highly advantageous for the people of the United States, while there is yet time, to read what the Belgian Minister in Berlin had to say on 27 October, 1905:

> A very large number of Germans are convinced that England is either seeking allies for an attack upon Germany, or else, which would be more in accordance with British tradition, that she is labouring to provoke a Continental war in which she would not join, but of which she would reap the profit.
>
> I am told that many English people are troubled with similar fears and go in dread of German aggression.
>
> I am puzzled upon what foundations such an impression in London can be based. Germany is absolutely incapable of attacking England. ...Are these people in England really sincere who go about expressing fears of a German invasion which could not materialize? Are they not rather pretending to be afraid of it in order to bring on a war which would annihilate

> Germany's navy, her merchant-fleet and her foreign commerce? Germany is as vulnerable to attack as England is safe from it; and if England were to attack Germany merely for the sake of extinguishing a rival, it would only be in accordance with her old precedents.
>
> In turn she wiped out the Dutch fleet, with the assistance of Louis XIV; then the French fleet; and the Danish fleet she even destroyed in time of peace and without any provocation, simply because it constituted a naval force of some magnitude.
>
> There are no ostensible grounds for war between Germany and England. The English hatred for Germany arises solely from jealousy of Germany's progress in shipping, in commerce and in manufacture.

Baron Greindl here presents an opinion very different from that in which the majority of Americans have been instructed; and before they accept further instruction at the hands of Viscount Bryce, they had better look into the matter somewhat for themselves.

Baron Greindl wrote the foregoing in October. In December, the head of the British Admiralty, Sir John Fisher, assured Colonel Repington that "Admiral Wilson's Channel fleet was alone strong enough to smash the whole

German fleet." *Two years* later, Sir John Fisher wrote to King Edward VII that "it is an absolute fact that Germany has not laid down a single dreadnaught, nor has she commenced building a single battleship or big cruiser for eighteen months.... England has ... ten dreadnaughts built and building, while Germany in March last had not even begun one dreadnaught ... we have 123 destroyers and forty submarines. The Germans have forty-eight destroyers and one submarine." Hence, if Sir John Fisher knew what he was talking about, and in such matters he usually did, he furnishes a very considerable corroboration of Baron Greindl's view of the German navy up to 1905. Looking back at the third chapter of this book, which deals with the comparative strength of the two navies and naval groups as developed from 1905 to 1914, the reader may well raise again Baron Greindl's question, "Are those people in England really sincere?"

XII

Such is the inveterate suspicion, the melancholy distrust, put upon English diplomacy by these foreign and neutral observers who could see so plainly what would befall their own country in the event of a European war. Such too, was the responsibility which these observers regularly imputed to the British Foreign Office—the British Foreign Office which was so soon to fix upon the neutrality of Belgium as a *casus belli* and pour out streams of propaganda about the sanctity of treaties and the rights of small nations! Every one of these observers exhibits this suspicion and distrust. In March, 1906, when Edward VII visited Paris and invited the discredited ex-Minister Delcassé to breakfast, the Belgian Minister at Paris wrote:

> It looks as though the king wished to demonstrate that the policy which called forth Germany's active intervention [over Morocco] has nevertheless remained unchanged.... In French circles it is not over well received; Frenchmen feeling that they are being dragged against their will in the orbit of English policy, a policy whose consequences they dread, and which they generally condemned by throwing over M. Delcassé. In short, people fear that this is a sign that

> England wants so to envenom the situation that war will become inevitable.

On 10 February, 1907, when the English King and Queen visited Paris, he says: "One can not conceal from oneself that these tactics, though their ostensible object is to prevent war, are likely to arouse great dissatisfaction in Berlin and to stir up a desire to risk anything that may enable Germany to burst the ring which England's policy is tightening around her." On 28 March, 1907, the Belgian *chargé d'affaires* in London speaks of "English diplomacy, whose whole effort is directed to the isolation of Germany." On the same date, by a curious coincidence, the Minister at Berlin, in the course of a blistering arraignment of French policy in Morocco, says: "But at the bottom of every settlement that has been made, or is going to be made, there lurks always that hatred of Germany.... It is a sequence of the campaign very cleverly conducted with the object of isolating Germany.... The English press is carrying on its campaign of calumny more implacably than ever. It sees the finger of Germany in everything that goes contrary to English wishes." On 18 April, 1907, Baron Greindl says of the King of England's visit to the King of Spain that, like the alliances with Japan and France and the negotiations with Russia, it is "one of the moves in the campaign to isolate Germany that is being personally directed with as much perseverance as success by His Majesty King Edward VII." In the same dispatch he remarks: "There is some right to regard with suspicion this eagerness to unite, for a so-called defensive object, Powers who are menaced by nobody. At Berlin they can not forget that offer of 100,000 men made by the King of England to M. Delcassé."

On 24 May, 1907, the Minister at London reported that "it is plain that official England is pursuing a policy that is covertly hostile, and tending to result in the isolation of Germany, and that King Edward has not been above putting his personal influence at the service of this cause." On 19 June, 1907, Count de Lalaing again writes from London of the Anglo-Franco-Spanish agreement concerning the *status quo* in the Mediterranean region, that "it is, however, difficult to imagine that Germany will not regard it as a further step in England's policy, which is determined, by every sort of means, to isolate the German Empire."

Perusal of these documents from beginning to end will show nothing to offset against the view of English diplomacy exhibited in the foregoing quotations; nothing to modify or qualify that view in any way. Baron Greindl, however, speaks highly of the British Ambassador at Berlin, Sir F. Lascelles, and praises his personal and unsupported attempt to establish friendly relations between England and Germany. Of this he says: "I have been a witness for the last twelve years of the efforts he has made to accomplish it. And yet, possessing as he justly does the absolute confidence of the Emperor and the German Government, and eminently gifted with the qualities of a statesman, he has nevertheless not succeeded very well so far." The next year, 1908, when Sir F. Lascelles was forced to resign his post, Baron Greindl does not hesitate to say that "the zeal with which he has worked to dispel misunderstandings that he thought absurd and highly mischievous for both countries, does not fall in with the political views of his sovereign."

XIII

King Edward VII died 6 May, 1910. During the early part of 1911, the Belgian Ministers in London, Paris and Berlin report some indications of a less unfriendly policy towards Germany on the part of the British Government. In March of that year, Sir Edward Grey delivered a reassuring speech on British foreign policy, on the occasion of the debate on the naval budget. The Belgian Minister in Berlin says of this that it should have produced the most agreeable impression in Germany if one could confidently believe that it really entirely reflected the ideas of the British Government. It would imply, he says, that "England no longer wishes to give to the Triple Entente the aggressive character which was stamped upon it by its creator, King Edward VII." He remarks, however, the slight effect produced in Berlin by Sir E. Grey's speech, and infers that German public feeling may have "become dulled by the innumerable meetings and mutual demonstrations of courtesy which have never produced any positive result," and he adds significantly that "this distrust is comprehensible."

It must be remembered that at the time this speech was delivered, England was under a secret agreement dating from 1904 to secure France's economic monopoly in Morocco. England was also under a secret obligation to France, dating from 1906, to support her in case of war with Germany. It must be above all remembered that this latter obligation carried with it a contingent liability for the Franco-Russian military alliance that had been in effect for many years. Thus if Russia went to war with Germany, France was committed, and in turn England was committed. The whole force of the Triple Entente lay in these agreements; and it can not be too often pointed out that they were *secret* agreements. No one in England knew until November, 1911, that in 1904 the British Government had bargained with the French Government, in return for a free hand in Egypt, to permit France to squeeze German economic interests out of Morocco—in violation of a published agreement, signed by all the interested nations, concerning the status of Morocco. No one in England knew until 3 August, 1914, that England had for several years been under a military and naval agreement with France which carried the enormous contingent liability of the Franco-Russian military alliance. No matter what appeared on the surface of politics; no matter how many pacific speeches were made by Sir E. Grey and Mr. Asquith, no matter what the newspapers said, no matter how often and how impressively Lord Haldane might visit Berlin in behalf of peace and good feeling; *those secret agreements held*, they were the only things that did hold, and everything worked out in strict accordance with them and with nothing else, least of all with any public understanding or any statement of policy put out for public consumption. It was just as in the subsequent case of the armistice and the peace—and this is something that has been far too little noticed in this country. The real terms of the armistice and of the peace were not the terms of the Fourteen Points or of any of the multitudinous published statements of Allied war aims. On the contrary, they were the precise terms of the secret treaties made among the Allied belligerents during the war, and made public on their discovery by the Soviet Government in the archives of the Tsarist Foreign Office.

It is no wonder then, that the German Government was not particularly impressed by Sir E. Grey's speech, especially as Germany saw France helping herself to Moroccan territory with both hands, and England looking on in indifferent complacency. In May, 1911, on a most transparent and preposterous pretext, a

French army was ordered to march on Fez, the capital of Morocco. The German Government then informed France that as the Algeciras Act, which guaranteed the integrity and independence of Morocco, had thereby gone by the board, Germany would no longer consider herself bound by its provisions. In June, 30,000 French troops "relieved" Fez, occupied it and stayed there, evincing no intention whatever of getting out again, notwithstanding that the ostensible purpose of the expedition was accomplished; in reality, there was nothing to accomplish. Two months before this *coup d'état*, Baron Greindl, the Belgian Minister at Berlin, wrote to the Belgian Foreign Office as follows:

> Every illusion, if ever entertained on the value of the Algeciras Act, which France signed with the firm intention of never observing, must long since have vanished. She has not ceased for one moment to pursue her plans of annexation; either by seizing opportunities for provisional occupations destined to last for ever or by extorting concessions which have placed the Sultan in a position of dependence upon France, and which have gradually lowered him to the level of the Bey of Tunis.

A week later, 29 April, Baron Guillaume, who had succeeded M. Leghait as Belgian Minister in Paris, reported that "there are, so far, no grounds for fearing that the French expedition will bring about any disturbance of international policy. Germany is a calm spectator of events." He adds, significantly, "England, having thrust France into the Moroccan bog, is contemplating her work with satisfaction."

France professed publicly that the object of this expedition was to extricate certain foreigners who were imperilled at Fez; and having done so, she would withdraw her forces. The precious crew of concessionaires, profiteers, and dividend-hunters known as the *Comité du Maroc* had suddenly discovered a whole French colony living in Fez in a state of terror and distress. There was, in fact, nothing of the sort. Fez was never menaced, it was never short of provisions, and there were no foreigners in trouble. When the expeditionary force arrived, it found no one to shoot at. As M. Francis de Pressensé says:

> Those redoubtable rebels who were threatening Fez had disappeared like dew in the morning. Barely did a few ragged horsemen fire off a shot or two before turning around and riding away at a furious gallop. A too disingenuous, or too truthful, correspondent gave the show away. The expeditionary force complains, he gravely records, of the absence of the enemy; the approaching harvest season is keeping all

> the healthy males in the fields! Thus did the phantom so dexterously conjured by the *Comité du Maroc* for the benefit of its aims, disappear in a night.

Nevertheless, the expeditionary force did not, in accordance with the public professions of the French Government, march out of Fez as soon as it discovered this ridiculous mare's nest. It remained there and held possession of the Moorish capital. What was the attitude of the British Government in the premises? On 2 May, in the House of Commons, Sir Edward Grey said that "the action taken by France is not intended to alter the political status of Morocco, and His Majesty's Government can not see why any objection should be taken to it."

Germany had remained for eight years a tolerant observer of French encroachments in Morocco, and quite clearly, as Baron Greindl observes in his report of 21 April, 1911, could not "after eight years of tolerance, change her attitude unless she were determined to go to war, and war is immeasurably more than Morocco is worth." In July, 1911, however, while the French force of 30,000 was still occupying Fez, Germany dispatched a gunboat, the *Panther*, which anchored off the coast of Agadir.

XIV

This was the famous "Agadir incident," of which we have all heard. Did it mean that the worm had turned, that Germany had changed her attitude and was determined to go to war? It has been so represented; but there are many difficult inconsistencies involved in that explanation of the German Government's act, and there is also an alternative explanation which fits the facts far better. In the first place the *Panther* was hardly more than an ocean-going tug. She was of 1000 tons burden, mounting two small naval guns, six machine-guns, and she carried a complement of only 125 men. Second, she never landed a man upon the coast of Morocco. She chose for her anchorage a point where the coast is practically inaccessible; Agadir has no harbour, and there is nothing near it that offers any possible temptation to the predatory instinct. No more ostentatiously unimpressive and unmenacing demonstration could have been devised. Germany, too, was quite well aware that Morocco was not worth a European war; and as Baron Guillaume said in his report of 29 April, "possibly she [Germany] is congratulating herself on the difficulties that weigh upon the shoulders of the French Government, and asks nothing better than to keep out of the whole affair as long as she is not forced into it by economic considerations." But the most significant indication that Germany had not changed her attitude is in the fact that if she were determined upon war, then, rather than two years later, was her time to go about it. This aspect of Germany's behaviour has been dealt with in a previous chapter. It can not be too often reiterated that if Germany really wanted war and was determined upon war, her failure to strike in 1908, when Russia was prostrate and France unready, and again in 1912, a few months after the Agadir incident, when the Balkan war was on, is inexplicable.[1]

[1]Critics of German foreign policy are hard put to it to show that she was ever guided by territorial ambitions; which is an extremely troublesome thing when one wants to believe that she proposed in 1914 to put the world under a military despotism. Can any one show where in a single instance she ever demanded anything more than economic equality with other nations, in a foreign market? Certainly she never demanded more than this in Morocco. Ex-Premier Caillaux says that his predecessor Rouvier offered Germany a good Moroccan port (Mogador) and some adjoining territory, and Germany declined.

The dispatch of the *Panther* gave the three Belgian observers a great surprise, and they were much puzzled to account for it. Baron Guillaume's thoughts at once turned to England. He writes 2 July:

> It was long regarded as an axiom that England would never allow the Germans to establish themselves at any point of Moroccan territory. Has this policy been abandoned; and if so, at what price were they bought off?

During the month of July, while waiting for a statement from the British Foreign Office, the Belgian observers canvassed the possibility that Germany's action was a hint that she would like some territorial compensation for having been bilked out of her share in the Moroccan market. But the interesting fact, and for the purpose of this book the important fact, is that none of these diplomats shows the slightest suspicion that Germany was bent on war or that she had any thought of going to war. Baron Guillaume says, 28 July, "undoubtedly the present situation wears a serious aspect.... Nobody, however, wants war, and they will try to avoid it." He proceeds:

> The French Government knows that a war would be the death-knell of the Republic.... I have very great confidence in the Emperor

> William's love of peace, notwithstanding the not infrequent air of melodrama about what he says and does.... Germany can not go to war for the sake of Morocco, nor yet to exact payment of those compensations that she very reasonably demands for the French occupation of Fez, which has become more or less permanent. On the whole I feel less faith in Great Britain's desire for peace. She would not be sorry to see the others destroying one another; only, under those circumstances, it would be difficult for her to avoid armed intervention.... As I thought from the very first, the crux of the situation is in London.

By the end of July, a different conception of Germany's action seemed to prevail. It began to be seen that the episode of the *Panther* had been staged by way of calling for a show-down on the actual intentions and purposes of the Triple Entente; and it got one. Mr. Lloyd George, "the impulsive Chancellor of the Exchequer," as Count de Lalaing calls him, made a typical jingo speech at the Mansion House; a speech which the Prime Minister, Mr. Asquith, and Sir Edward Grey, the Foreign Minister, had helped him to compose. The air was cleared at once—England stood by France—and what better plan could have been devised for clearing the air than the dispatch of the *Panther*? Germany stood for the policy of economic equality, the policy of the open door to which all the Powers interested had agreed in the case of Morocco. France, at the end of a course of continuous aggression, had put 30,000 troops in occupation of the capital of Morocco on an infamously unscrupulous pretext, and put them there to stay, and the British Government "could not see why any objection should be taken to it." Germany, on the other hand, anchored an insignificant gunboat off an inaccessible coast, and without landing a man or firing a shot, left her there as a silent reminder of the Algeciras Act and the principle of the open door—carefully and even ostentatiously going no further—and the British Government promptly, through the mouth of Mr. Lloyd George, laid down a challenge and a threat. Thereupon Germany and France understood their relative positions; they understood, even without Sir E. Grey's explicit reaffirmation of 27 November of the policy of the Triple Entente, that England would stand by her arrangements with France. Baron Greindl writes from Berlin 6 December, and puts the case explicitly:

> Was it not assuming the right of veto on German enterprise for England to start a hue and cry because a German cruiser cast anchor in the roads of Agadir, seeing that she had looked on without a murmur whilst France and Spain had

proceeded step by step to conquer Morocco and to destroy the independence of its Sultan?

England could not have acted otherwise. She was tied by her secret treaty with France. The explanation was extremely simple, but it was not of a sort to allay German irritation.

XV

Let us glance at British political chronology for a moment. King Edward VII, the chief factor in the Entente, the moving spirit in England's foreign alliances, had been dead a year. In December, 1905, the Liberal party had come into power. In April, 1908, Mr. H. H. Asquith became Prime Minister. In 1910, Anglo-German relations were apparently improving; in July, 1910, Mr. Asquith spoke of them in the House of Commons as "of the most cordial character. I look forward to increasing warmth and fervour and intimacy in these relations year by year." The great question was, then, in 1911, whether the Liberal Government would actually, when it came down to the pinch, stick by its secret covenant with France. Were the new Liberals, were Mr. Asquith, Lord Haldane, Sir E. Grey, Mr. Lloyd George, true-blue Liberal imperialists, or were they not? Could France and Russia safely trust them to continue the Foreign Office policy that Lord Lansdowne had bequeathed to Sir E. Grey; or, when the emergency came, would they stand from under? After all, there *had* been a Campbell-Bannerman; there was no doubt of that; and one, at least, of the new Liberals, Mr. Lloyd George, had a bad anti-imperialist record in the South African war.

The Agadir incident elicited a satisfactory answer to these questions. The Liberal Government was dependable. However suspiciously the members of the Liberal Cabinet might talk, they were good staunch imperialists at heart. They were, as the theologians say, "sound on the essentials." Baron Greindl wrote, 6 December, 1911:

> The Entente Cordiale was founded, not on the positive basis of defence of common interests, but on the negative one of hatred of the German Empire.... Sir Edward Grey adopts this tradition without reservation. He imagines that it is in conformity with English interests.... A revision of Great Britain's policy is all the less to be looked for, as ever since the Liberal Ministry took office, and more especially during the last few months, English foreign policy has been guided by the ideas with which King Edward VII inspired it.

XVI

Mr. Lloyd George's speech at the Mansion House in July, 1911, after the German gunboat *Panther* had anchored off the Moroccan coast, gave an immense impulse to the jingo spirit in France, because it was taken as definite assurance of England's good faith in seeing her secret agreements through to a finish. M. Caillaux, the French Premier, appears to have had his doubts, nevertheless, inasmuch as the British Foreign Office did not give a straight reply to the French Foreign Office's inquiry concerning British action in case the Germans landed a force in Morocco. He says:

> Are we to understand that our powerful neighbours will go right through to the end with the resolve which they suggest? Are they ready for all eventualities? The British Ambassador, Sir Francis Bertie, with whom I converse, does not give me formal assurances. It is said, of course, that he would see without displeasure the outbreak of a conflict between France and Germany; his mind works in the way attributed to a number of leading British officials at the Foreign Office.

M. Caillaux here suggests the same suspicion of British intentions which the Belgian diplomats at London, Paris and Berlin intimate continually throughout their correspondence since 1905.[1] He accordingly favoured a less energetic policy towards Germany, and was thrown out of office. Count de Lalaing reported from London, 15 January, 1912, that the revelations which provoked this political crisis were disagreeable for the English Government. "They seem to prove," he says, "that the French Premier had been trying to negotiate with Berlin without the knowledge of the Minister for Foreign Affairs and his other colleagues, and this is naturally disquieting to a Government whose interests are bound up with those of France, and which accordingly can ill tolerate any lapses of this kind." He adds:

> These revelations have also strengthened the impression that M. Caillaux had recently favoured an ultra-conciliatory policy towards Germany, and this impression was felt all the more painfully in English official circles, as the full extent of the tension between London and Berlin caused by the Cabinet of St. James's loyal behaviour towards the Cabinet at Paris had hardly been grasped. People in England are reluctant to face the fact that they have been 'more royalist than the King,' and have shown themselves

[1] This is worth noticing since M. Caillaux was the pioneer victim of the charge of being "pro-German."

> even less accommodating than the friend they were backing.... Accordingly the press unanimously hails with delight the departure of M. Caillaux, and trusts that sounder traditions may be reverted to without delay.

This comment on the position of M. Caillaux is one of the most interesting observations to be found in these documents.

XVII

THE Balkan war took place in 1912, and the whole history of the year shows the most mighty efforts of European politicians—efforts which seem ludicrous and laughable in spite of their tragic quality—to avert with their left hand the war which they were bringing on with their right. Mr. Lloyd George is right in saying that no one really wanted war. What every one wanted, and what every one was trying with might and main to do, was to cook the omelette of economic imperialism without breaking any eggs. There was in all the countries, naturally, a jingo nationalist party which wanted war. In Russia, which was then busily reorganizing her military forces which had been used up and left prostrate by the war with the Japanese, the pan-Slavists were influential and vociferous, but they were not on top. In England there was a great popular revulsion against the behaviour of the Government which had so nearly involved the English in a war against Germany the year before; and Mr. Asquith's Government, which was pacifist in tendency, was meeting the popular sentiment in every way possible, *short of the one point of revealing the secret engagements which bound it to the French Government and contingently to the Russian Government.* Lord Haldane undertook an official mission to Berlin, which was attended with great publicity and was popularly supposed to be of a pacificatory nature; and really, within the limits of the Franco-English diplomatic agreement, it went as far as it could in the establishment of good relations. In fact, of course, it came to nothing; as long as the diplomatic agreement remained in force, it could come to nothing, nothing of the sort could come to anything; and the diplomatic agreement being guarded as a close secret, the reason why it must come to nothing was not apparent. The German Government also made tremendous efforts in behalf of peace; and it must be noted by those who accept the theory upon which the treaty of Versailles is based, that if Germany had wished or intended at any time to strike at the peace of Europe, now was the moment for her to do so. Instead, the German Emperor in person, and the German Government, through one of its best diplomatic agents, Baron von Marschall, met every pacific overture more than half-way, and themselves initiated all that could be thought of. "There is no doubt," wrote Baron Beyens from Berlin, "that the Emperor, the Chancellor and the Secretary of State for Foreign Affairs (von Kiderlen-Wächter) are passionately pacifists." Baron Beyens again says, 28 June, 1912, "The Emperor is persistent and has not given up hopes of winning back English sympathies, just as he has succeeded up to a certain point in obtaining the confidence of the Tsar, by the force of his personal attractions." Those who believe in the extraordinary notion of an unprepared and unsuspecting Europe, should read the diplomatic history of the year 1912, when all the chief officeholders in England and on the Continent were struggling like men caught in a quicksand, or like flies on fly-paper, to avert, or if they could not avert, to defer the inevitable war.

In one country, however, the jingo nationalist and militarist party came on top; and that country was France. M. Caillaux was succeeded by Raymond Poincaré; and in January, 1913, Poincaré became President of the Republic. Up to 1912, the people of France were increasingly indisposed to war and were developing a considerable impatience with militarism, and the French Government was responsive to this sentiment. It knew, as Baron Guillaume remarked at the time of the Agadir incident, that "a war would be the death-knell of the Republic." M. Caillaux seems to have measured the feelings of his countrymen quite well. Baron Guillaume says that after the dispatch of the *Panther*, the British Cabinet's first proposal was that the British and French Governments should each immediately send two men-of-war to Agadir; and that the French Cabinet strongly objected. Again, he says in his report of 8 July, 1911, "I am persuaded that Messrs. Caillaux and de Selves regret the turn given to the Moroccan affair by their predecessors in office. They were quite ready to give way, provided they could do so without humiliation."

The speech of Mr. Lloyd George at the Mansion House, however, which was taken by the French (and how correctly they took it became apparent on 3 August, 1914) as a definite assurance of British support against Germany, gave the militarist-nationalist party the encouragement to go ahead and dominate the domestic politics of France. It put the Poincaré–Millerand–Delcassé element on its feet and stiffened its resolution, besides clearing the way in large measure for its predominance. On 14 February, 1913, Baron Guillaume reports from Paris thus:

> The new President of the Republic enjoys a popularity in France to-day unknown to any of his predecessors.... Various factors contribute to explain his popularity. His election had been carefully prepared in advance; people are pleased at the skilful way in which, while a Minister, he

manœuvred to bring France to the fore in the concert of Europe; he has hit upon some happy phrases that stick in the popular mind.

The career of M. Poincaré, in fact, and his management of popular sentiment, show many features which *mutatis mutandis*, find a parallel in the career of Theodore Roosevelt. Baron Guillaume adds, however, this extremely striking observation concerning the popularity of M. Poincaré:

> But above all, one must regard it as a manifestation of the old French chauvinistic spirit, which had for many years slumbered, but which had come to life again since the affair of Agadir.

In the same communication to the Belgian Foreign Office, Baron Guillaume remarks:

> M. Poincaré is a native of Lorraine, and loses no opportunity of telling people so. He was M. Millerand's colleague, and the instigator of his militarist policy.
>
> Finally, the first word that he uttered at the very moment when he learned that he was elected President of the Republic, was a promise that he would watch over and maintain all the means of national defence.

M. Poincaré had not been in office two months when he recalled the French Ambassador at Petersburg, M. Georges Louis, and appointed in his stead M. Delcassé. Concerning this stupendous move, Baron Guillaume reported 21 February, 1913, to the Belgian Foreign Office thus:

> The news that M. Delcassé is shortly to be appointed Ambassador at Petersburg burst like a bomb here yesterday afternoon.... He was one of the architects of the Franco-Russian alliance, and still more so of the Anglo-French *entente.*

Baron Guillaume goes on to say that he does not think that M. Delcassé's appointment should be interpreted as a demonstration against Germany; but he adds:

> I do think, however, that M. Poincaré, a Lorrainer, was not sorry to show, from the first day of entering on his high office, how anxious he is to stand firm and hold aloft the national flag. That is the danger involved in having M. Poincaré at the Elysée in these anxious days through which Europe is passing. It was under his Ministry that the militarist, slightly bellicose instincts of the French woke up again. He has been thought to have a measure of responsibility for this change of mood.

M. Georges Louis, who had represented the French Government at Petersburg for three years, was a resolute opponent of the militarist faction in France, and was therefore distinctly *persona non grata* to the corresponding faction in Russia. At the head of this faction stood Isvolsky, who was a friend of M. Poincaré and a kindred spirit; hence when M. Poincaré became Premier, an attempt was made to oust M. Louis, but it was unsuccessful. M. Delcassé, on the other hand, is described by Mr. Morel as "the man identified more than any other man in French public life with the anti-German war-party." Mr. Morel, in commenting on the appointment of M. Delcassé quotes the following from a report sent by the Russian Ambassador in London to the Foreign Office in Petersburg. It was written four days after the appointment of M. Delcassé, and quite bears out the impression made upon the Belgian agents.[1]

> When I recall his [M. Cambon, the French Ambassador in London] conversations with me, and the attitude of Poincaré, the thought comes to me as a conviction, that of all the powers France is the only one which, not to say that it wishes war, would yet look upon it without great regret....She [France] has, either rightly or wrongly, complete trust in her army; the old effervescing minority has again shown itself.

[1]But perhaps Count Beuckendorf was pro-German, too!

XVIII

The French war-party, represented by MM. Poincaré, Millerand and Delcassé, came into political predominance in January, 1912, and consolidated its ascendancy one year later, when M. Raymond Poincaré became President of the French Republic. All through 1912 there was an immense amount of correspondence and consultation between the French and Russian Governments, and all through 1913 Russia showed extraordinary activity in military preparation. In England, Mr. Asquith's Government had to face a strong revulsion of popular feeling against the attitude of its diplomacy, which had so nearly involved the country in war with Germany at the time of the Agadir incident.

As always, the figures of expenditure tell the story; and the history of 1912–14 should be continually illustrated by reference to the financial statistics of the period, which have been given in earlier chapters. For instance, Russia, which spent (in round numbers) £3¼ million on new naval construction in 1911, spent £7 million in 1912, £12 million in 1913, and £13 million in 1914. The fact that, as Professor Raymond Beazley puts it, in the ten years before the war, and with increasing insistence, Paris and St. Petersburg spent upon armaments £159 million more than Berlin or Vienna, ought to suffice at least to reopen the question of responsibility.

It must be carefully noted that by the spring of 1912, the Balkan League, which was engineered by the Russian diplomat Hartwig, was fully formed. This put the diplomacy of the Balkan States under the direct control of the Russian Foreign Office. It now became necessary for the Russian Foreign Office to ascertain, in case war between Serbia and Austria broke out, and Germany should help Austria and Russia should help Serbia, whether Russia could count on the support of France and England. Russia received this assurance in secret, and the terms of it were discovered by the Soviet Government in the archives of the Foreign Office and published in 1919. This is a most important fact, and should be continually borne in mind in connexion with the fact that the war was precipitated by the murder of the Austrian Archduke by Serbian officers, members of the pan-Slavist organization fostered and encouraged by MM. Isvolsky and Hartwig.

On 9 August, 1912, M. Poincaré, then Premier of France, made a visit to St. Petersburg, where he was joined by his kindred spirit, M. Isvolsky, who was then the Russian Ambassador at Paris. It was the usual visit of State, and Russia staged an imposing series of military manœuvres in M. Poincaré's honour. But the really important events that took place were these. First, a naval agreement was made between France and Russia, whereby France agreed to concentrate her naval forces in the Eastern Mediterranean in order to support the Russian navy in the Black Sea. This agreement was secret, and revealed by the Soviet Government in 1918. Then, in the same month, the Third French Naval Squadron was transferred from the Atlantic to the Mediterranean. M. Poincaré told M. Isvolsky that "this decision has been made in agreement with England, and forms the further development and completion of the arrangement already made previously between the French and British Staffs"—referring to the conference of Messrs. Asquith and Churchill and Lord Kitchener at Malta, the month before, at which the new disposition of the English and French fleets was decided. The third matter of consequence that took place in the month of August was that the Russian Government began to put pressure on the French Government to re-establish the Three Years Military Service law.

So much for August. In the month of September, M. Poincaré gave the Russian Foreign Minister, M. Sazonov, assurance that if Germany helped Austria in a struggle in the Balkans, and if Russia were drawn in on the other side, France "would not hesitate for a moment to fulfil its obligations towards Russia." In the same month, M. Isvolsky had an interview with the King of England and Sir Edward Grey, the British Foreign Minister, in which both King George and Sir E. Grey assured him of the fullest British co-operation in the same event. M. Isvolsky reported to the Russian Foreign Office at St. Petersburg, that "Grey, upon his own initiative, corroborated what I already knew from Poincaré—the existence of an agreement between France and Great Britain, according to which England undertook, in case of a war with Germany, not only to come to the assistance of France on the sea, but also on the Continent, by landing troops." These two understandings between MM. Poincaré and Sazonov, and between M. Isvolsky and Sir E. Grey, were secret, and nothing was known of them until 1919, when the memoranda of them were published by the Soviet Government.[1]

[1]On 10 March of the following year, Mr. Asquith,

A train of gunpowder, in other words, had been laid from Belgrade through Paris and Lon-

---

replying to a question in the Commons from Lord Hugh Cecil, denied that England was under an "obligation arising owing to an assurance given by the Ministry in the course of diplomatic negotiations, to send a very large armed force out of this country to operate in Europe." On 24 March, he made similar denials in reply to questions from Sir W. Byles and Mr. King. On 14 April, Mr. Runciman, in a speech at Birkenhead, denied "in the most categorical way" the existence of a secret understanding with any foreign Power! On 3 May, the Secretary for the Colonies, Mr. Harcourt, declared publicly that he "could conceive no circumstances in which Continental operations would not be a crime against the people of this country." On 28 June, the under-Secretary for Foreign Affairs, Mr. Acland, declared publicly that "in no European question were we concerned to interfere with a big army." On 1 July, Lord Loreburn, Lord Chancellor from 1906 to 1912, said "that any British Government would be so guilty towards our country as to take up arms in a foreign quarrel is more than I can believe." On 28 April, 1914, and again on 11 June, Sir E. Grey confirmed, in the House of Commons, Mr. Asquith's assertion, made 10 and 24 March, 1913, of British freedom from engagements with Continental Powers.

Yet, curiously the professions of politicians are still trusted, and people still expect something from their machinations; they expected something substantial from the recent conference in Washington, on the limitation of armaments, for instance—a striking and pathetic example of the strength of superstition.

don to St. Petersburg; and at the beginning of that train was the highly inflammable and inflammatory pan-Slavism, organized by M. Hartwig with the connivance of M. Isvolsky. A spark struck in the Balkans would cause the train to flash into flame throughout its entire length.

XIX

On 25 April, 1912, the German Reichstag put through its first reading a bill, with only perfunctory debate, for an increase in the German army and navy. This measure has been regularly and officially interpreted as a threat. Yet nearly a year after, on 19 February, 1913, Baron Guillaume, writing from Paris about the prospects of the Three Years Service bill, reports to the Belgian Foreign Office that the French Minister of War "does not regard the measures taken by Germany as a demonstration of hostility, but rather as an act of prudence for the future. Germany fears that she may one day have to fight Russia and France together, perhaps England too; and then any help that Austria might give her would be seriously handicapped by the fact that the Dual Monarchy [Austria-Hungary] would have to withstand a coalition of Balkan States."

Naturally. The bill was presented to the Reichstag in April, and the "coalition of Balkan States," M. Hartwig's Balkan League, had already completed its organization in February. Not only so, but the very first step taken by this exemplary organization provided for a division of spoils in the event of a successful war with Turkey; and six months after the organization of the League was concluded, it served an ultimatum upon Turkey over Albania, and in October went to war. The German Government could quite plainly see the future about to be inaugurated through this consolidation of Balkan policy into the hands of the Russian Foreign Office—any one even an attentive reader of newspapers, could see it—and it could see the vastly increased responsibility of its Austrian ally, in case of a quarrel, should it have to take on a coalition of the Balkan States instead of a single one.

Count de Lalaing reported from London, 24 February, 1918, that the British Foreign Office took the same sensible view of the German military increases as, according to Baron Guillaume, was taken by M. Jonnart. "The English press," he says, "is of course anxious to saddle Germany with the responsibility for the fresh tension caused by her schemes—a tension which may give Europe fresh reasons for uneasiness." But, he goes on—

> At the Foreign Office I found a more equitable and calmer estimate of the situation. They see in the reinforcement of the German armies not so much a provocation as an admission

> that circumstances have weakened Germany's military position, and that it must be strengthened. The Berlin Government is compelled to recognize that it can no longer count upon being supported by the whole force of its Austrian ally, now that a new Power, that of the Balkan Federation, has made its appearance in South-eastern Europe, right at the gates of the Dual Empire.... Under these circumstances, the Foreign Office sees nothing astonishing in Germany's finding it imperative to increase the number of her army corps. The Foreign Office also states that the Berlin Government had told the Paris Cabinet quite frankly that such were the motives for its action.

The same view was publicly expressed by Mr. Lloyd George himself as late as 1 January, 1914, when he said:

> The German army was vital, not merely to the existence of the German Empire, but to the very life and independence of the nation itself, surrounded, as Germany is, by other nations, each of which possesses armies as powerful as her own. We forget that while we insist upon a sixty-per-cent superiority (as far as our naval strength is concerned) over Germany being essential to guarantee the integrity of our own shores, Germany herself has nothing like that superiority over France alone, and she has of

> course, in addition, to reckon with Russia on her eastern frontier. Germany has nothing which approximates to a two-Power standard. She has, therefore, become alarmed by recent issues, and is spending huge sums of money on the expansion of her military resources.

Those are the words, be it remembered, of the same person who says to-day that German responsibility for the war which broke out six months after he had made the foregoing statement, is a *chose jugée*! The statement was made, furthermore, not only after the German bill of 25 April, 1912, but *after* the bill of 8 April, 1913, as well, which fixed the peace-strength of the German army at 870,000.

The Three Years Service law passed the French Chamber in August, 1913, after a passionate popular campaign. Of this measure Baron Guillaume says that the French newspapers, *Le Temps* in particular, "are wrong in representing the French Government's plans as being in response to measures adopted by Germany. Many of them are but the outcome of measures which have long been prepared." The French Minister, M. Jonnart, told him that "we know very well what an advantage our neighbour [Germany] has in the continual growth of his population; still, we must do all that lies in our power to compensate this advantage by better military organization." Probably this view of the Three Years Service law was the view held by all save the relatively small and highly-integrated war-faction; and in so far as military measures are ever reasonable, this, like the corresponding measures taken in Germany, must be regarded as reasonable. As M. Pichon told Baron Guillaume, "We are not arming for war, we are arming to avoid it, to exorcise it.... We must go on arming more and more in order to prevent war." There is no reason whatever to suppose that this view was not sincerely entertained by M. Pichon and by many others, probably by a majority of the persons most responsibly concerned.

But the consequences of the Three Years Service law were contemplated by Baron Guillaume with great apprehension. He reports on 12 June, 1913, that "the burden of the new law will fall so heavily upon the population, and the expenditure which it will involve will be so exorbitant, that there will soon be an outcry in the country, and France will be faced with this dilemma: either renounce what she can not bear to forgo, or else, war at short notice." Of the militarist party now in the ascendancy, he says: "They are followed with a sort of infatuation, a kind of frenzy which is interesting but deplorable. One is not now allowed, under pain of being marked as a traitor, to express even a doubt of the need for the Three Years Service."

Public opinion was evidently confiscated by the Poincaré–Millerand–Delcassé group, much as it was in the United States in 1917 by the war-party headed by Mr. Wilson. Baron Guillaume uses words that must remind us of those days. "Every one knows," he says, "that the mass of the nation is by no means in favour of the projected reform, and they understand the danger that lies ahead. But they shut their eyes and press on."

XX

The train of powder, however, had been laid by the diplomatic engagements. Austria-Hungary and Serbia came into collision in the spring of 1913 over the Scutari incident. In December, 1912, M. Sazonov had urged Serbia to play a waiting game in order to "deliver a blow at Austria." But on 4 April, 1913, Baron Beyens reports from Berlin that the arrogance and contempt with which the Serbs receive the Vienna Cabinet's protests over Scutari

> can only be explained by their belief that St. Petersburg will support them. The Serbian chargé d'affaires was quite openly saying here lately that his Government would not have persisted in its course for the last six months in the face of the Austrian opposition had they not received encouragement in their course from the Russian Minister, M. de Hartwig, who is a diplomatist of M. Isvolsky's school.... M. Sazonov's heart is with his colleagues who are directing the policy of the Great Powers, but he feels his influence with the Tsar being undermined by the court-party and the pan-Slavists. Hence his inconsequent behaviour.

The military activity which the Russian Government displayed in 1913 gives interest to this estimate of M. Sazonov's position. No doubt to some extent the estimate was correct; M. Sazonov, like Sir E. Grey, was probably, when it was too late, much disquieted by the events which marshalled him the way that he was going. In 1914, this military activity gained extraordinary intensity. The Russian army was put upon a peace-footing of approximately 1,400,000, "an effective numerical strength hitherto unprecedented," said the St. Petersburg correspondent of the London *Times.* From January to June, the Russian Government made immense purchases of war material. In February, it concluded a loan in Paris for the improvement of its strategic roads and railways on the German frontier. Russia, as was generally known at the time, had her eye on the acquisition of Constantinople; and in the same month, February, a council of war was held in St. Petersburg to work out "a general programme of action in order to secure for us a favourable solution of the historical question of the Straits." In March, the St. Petersburg newspaper which served as the mouthpiece of the Minister of War, published an article stating that Russia's strategy would no longer be "defensive" but "active." Another paper spoke of the time coming when "the crossing of the Austrian frontier by the Russian army would be an unavoidable decision." In the same month, Russia raised a heavy tariff against the importation of German grain and flour; thus bearing out the evidence of German trade-reports that even at this time Germany was still exporting grain to Russia—a most extraordinary proceeding for a nation which contemplated a sudden declaration of war before the next harvest. In the same month, the Russian Government brought in military estimates of £97 million. It exercised heavy pressure on the French Government in the protracted political turmoil over the maintenance of the Three Years Service law. In April, "trial mobilizations" were begun, and were continued up to the outbreak of the war. In May, M. Sazonov informed the Tsar that the British Government "has decided to empower the British Admiralty Staff to enter into negotiations with French and Russian naval agents in London for the purpose of drawing technical conditions for possible action by the naval forces of England, Russia and France." In the same month, a complete mobilization of all the reserves of the three annual contingents of 1907–1909 was ordered for the whole Russian Empire, as a "test," to take place in the autumn. In the same month the Russian Admiralty instructed its agent in London, Captain Volkov, as follows:

> Our interests on the Northern scene of operations require that England keeps as large a part of the German fleet as possible in check

> in the North Sea....The English Government could render us a substantial service if it would agree to send a sufficient number of boats to our Baltic ports to compensate for our lack of means of transport, before the beginning of war-operations.

This document, revealed by the Soviet Government in 1919, is pretty damaging to the assumption of an "unprepared and unsuspecting Europe"; especially as Professor Conybeare has given publicity to the fact that "before the beginning of war-operations" those English boats were there, prompt to the minute, empty, ready and waiting.

In June, the Russian Ambassador warned the Russian naval staff in London that they must exercise great caution in talking about a landing in Pomerania or about the dispatch of English boats to the Russian Baltic ports before the outbreak of war, "so that the rest may not be jeopardized." On 13 June, the newspaper-organ of the Russian Minister of War published an inspired article under the caption: "Russia is Ready: France must be Ready."

Two weeks later, the Austrian heir-apparent, the Archduke Francis Joseph, was murdered at Sarajevo, a town in Bosnia, by Serbian officers. The murder was arranged by the Serbian

Major Tankesitch, of the pan-Slavist organization known as the Black Hand; and this organization was fostered, if not actually subsidized, by the Russian Minister at Belgrade, M. Hartwig, the pupil and *alter ego* of M. Isvolsky, and the architect and promoter of the Balkan League!